Today I liberate myself

Surviving the Unthinkable

Table of Contents

Go download and secure your free Workbook!

I created this because I believe it would be a great addition to keep you as the reader engaged in my book by allowing you to elaborate or remix some of my ideas or thoughts.

Go to
www.marcusbowen.net/LTBGworkbook
to download your FREE workbook today!

May Your Soul Rest in Paradise
Mambacita!

I'm dedicating pages 2,8, & 24 to my idols and those lost in that horrific accident on January 26th, 2020.

Dear LiL Bo,

10/06/2004

When I am I smile and laft. I like to play games and go out side. I like to watch T.V. and lay down. Sometimes I color when I am happy. When at the movies sometimes I am happy. When jump up and down I am happy. When I go to my baseball game I am happy. When I go to UCF game or Jags I am happy. When I get good grades I am happy. When I be a patrol I am happy. When I see my family members I am happy. When it is the holidays I'm happy. Everything I do good I'm happy.

Sincerely,

Eleven-year-old Marcus Bowen

This book has indeed been a journey. Since you are reading it, I want you to know you are beautiful; keep fighting the good fight. Hard work does pay off. My writing skills were awful in 2004 yet I was determined to write this book and here it is.

I do not have all the answers but I can tell you a little about my life and how I gained insight from my experiences growing up. So, please read my thoughts with me and don't be afraid to read them with a sarcastic voice. Enjoy!

Peace, Love & Happiness

ANCESTRAL POWERS

We must continue to stand up and fight for what's right. Our ancestors didn't take those lashes in vain. They took them because they knew one day our time would come. And that time is now. We will no longer be subjugated to beast and animals. We will look our oppressors in their eyes and tell them we will no longer take their hate. We will finish what our Ancestors started. I AM YOUNG, BLACK, AND GIFTED; AND YOU ARE TOO! DON'T YOU EVER FORGET THAT.

TODAY, I LIBERATE MYSELF FROM THESE SHACKLES!

TODAY, I FREE MY SOUL FROM THIS CAGE!

**AND TODAY, I SPEAK MY TRUTH
TO THE BEST OF MY ABILITIES!**

JUNE 19, 1865 -JUNE 19, 2020

PRELUDE

You must be wondering why I wrote this. Well, I'm a creator and I have the power to do so. AND DEEP DOWN INSIDE YOU HAVE THAT POWER TOO. You must have the utmost belief in thyself. This practice (the affirmations) are for you and your trillions of cells. Having an attitude of gratitude is especially important. It may not seem like it but this simple practice can have a tremendous impact on your life. These affirmations allowed me to slowly get rid of my negative thoughts. So, please read each one; don't skip over them and enjoy.

TO MY THREE MAGNOLIA FLOWERS
YOU TAUGHT ME EVERYTHING
YOUR STRENGTH TAUGHT ME EVEN MORE
WOMEN DESERVE TO BE TREATED EQUALLY
ARGUE WITH YOURSELF IN THE MIRROR

i love myself, I love myself;
I LOVE MYSELF!
i love myself, I love myself;
I LOVE MYSELF!
i love myself, I love myself;
I LOVE MYSELF!
I'm Thankful to see
another day!
I'm Thankful to see
another day!
I'M THANKFUL TO SEE
ANOTHER DAY!
I am greater than my obstacles!
I am greater than my obstacles!
I AM GREATER THAN MY
OBSTACLES!

Mamba Mentality

SELF LOVE

IT STARTS FROM WITHIN. LOVE IS THE MOST POWERFUL THING ON THIS UNIVERSE.

Learning to love yourself to the best of your ability can genuinely help you get over life's hardships. But you must be willing to opening your heart; and you must understand the power you hold to control your narrative. Equanimity is the word. Maintaining mental or emotional stability or composure, especially under tension or strain; calmness; equilibrium is the definition. Learn to live by that and no one will be able to knock you off the Love Train. When you learn to channel this state of Love, you start to live in a realm of positivity and focus only on the positives in life. You will grow to understand that a negative environment – which once controlled your state of Love - can no longer do that.

I have learned to love myself more than recording artist Kanye West loves Kanye West. By learning to love myself, I was able to love others in ways I couldn't before. I realized that I wasn't the only one who had problems; what I was learning was that despite them I must try my best to be compassionate and understanding. We all should. So, whenever I'm around people, I try my best to be a loving and kind person treating everyone I come across with the same love and respect. Self-love helped me become more empathetic, more compassionate, and more eager to help others. I didn't want people to struggle as I did in the past.

I had a lot of self-hate and insecurities. It all began at an early age; the age of eight to be exact. I hear you - tell us already! Okay, okay, I will. When I was eight my best friend molested me. We did everything together but we had never done that. That was the worst night of my life and has to date been the lowest point of my life.

I remember the tragedy like it was yesterday. Our favorite song was "Big Poppa" by hip hop artist Biggie Smalls. We would sing while we played. We'd come in from being outside playing and were getting ready for bed. We got on our knees and said our prayers; the things we usually did.

About thirty to forty-five minutes after we climbed into bed, I started to feel a wet sensation around my penis. I was the kid that when sex scenes came on, I would cover my eyes. At that age, I wasn't thinking about sex at all. I didn't like what he was doing to me. I started crying and told him to stop multiple times but he didn't.

I felt betrayed and it haunted me for most of my life. After that traumatic experience, I let my environment control me. I blamed others for how I acted instead of blaming myself. I would allow negativity to control my emotions and actions; I was good at hiding it. I was the kid who was always smiling no matter what. In public, no one could see my pain.

It was when I was alone that things would make a turn for the worse. I would look in the mirror and be disgusted with myself. I remember my mom took me to the store and these older ladies complimented me on my long eyelashes, and as soon as I got home, I cut them off because I was embarrassed that my eyelashes were regarded as beautiful, which was seen as feminine in my eyes. As for the friend who molested me; we didn't live in the same state, and as I got older, I distanced myself from him and eventually cut him off. I never hated him for what he did but I also didn't want anything to do with him.

I was in that dark place until I was 22 years old. I would constantly cry and beg for the Lord to take my life. I had fallen into the abyss, and for the longest, it looked like I wasn't going to escape. I could have won an Oscar for keeping the darkness at bay while I was around others.

I finally broke down and told my parents when I was 22. My parents were in shock and couldn't believe what had happened to me as a child. They wanted me to seek help and not be afraid to talk to them. I shared with them that I was afraid to tell them what had happened to me because as a kid I didn't know how they would have responded. I had been silent for fourteen long years and getting that off my chest was such an amazing feeling. I no longer felt the weight of the world within. From that moment on, I took an oath to better myself, and it has been a journey, an amazing one at that.

It's kind of hard to explain but after making a conscious effort to love myself, which started shortly after, I told my parents what happened. Releasing that negative energy helped me realize I wasn't properly taking care of myself and I needed to change for the better. I started gaining the ability to feel people's energies. It was like I could sense if someone was hurting or hiding their pain. My awareness started to grow. I would have heart felt conversations with strangers. You'd be surprised on how impactful it is to live a life of agape (which means unconditional love). Just treating everyone with the same respect you would want to be treated; no matter how ugly a situation, relationship or partnership might become or is. The same applies to loving someone simply because they are human regardless of your opinion on their status.

I went to a chemistry event at Barry University and noticed the teacher's assistant was there. Prior to the event she hadn't shown up to our class to assist. I could feel her spirit was troubled. She ended up being on my Brain Bawl Team (we were playing jeopardy). Me being me since I've found my true Love for life, it was one of my passions to spread the knowledge to help other's get over their pain. So, during that event I would joke around and be like "you have to get your chakra's aligned and that Love is the most powerful thing in this world." I had made it my mission to cheer her up and put a smile on her face. I knew it had to be a reason why she hadn't shown up for class for the past week. Doing whatever it took to make sure she was comfortable and enjoying her time at the event was my mission.

The whole time she's looking at me as if I'm a crazy person. It seemed like speaking from the heart was rare. The event ended and I decided to walk her to her car. That's when I felt obligated to ask, "What's wrong?"

She was like; "Wait. What? How do you know I'm hurting?"

I told her: "I have become one with myself because of all the meditation I do. God sent me to let you know that everything will be okay; but, you have to want to be better. You can't let people deter you from your greatness." I shared that I had battled what she was battling. She broke down in tears and I finally realized that what I was joking around about was indeed true.

She said; "You don't know how much I needed this." I was using my Love to help others find their Love. If you suppress Storge/affection, you suppress Philia/friendship, Eros/romance, and Agape/unconditional Love. It wasn't until I took an ethics course at Barry University to fully appreciate the four different types of love. Was this a sign from God showing me I was ready to learn more? I believed so, and I grew to like this breakdown because the word love is so broad.

Storge, the most basic of the four, is what we see on a daily basis, which is affection. It's the type of love you would give to a pet. But it's a type of love we should be open to share with every and anyone.

Philia is our next type of love, and if you heard or knew of Philadelphia, the city of brotherly love then it is easy for you to connect the dots like I did. As soon as I saw Philia, Philadelphia came to the front of my mind, and I immediately had a feeling of what it meant - which is friendship. Throughout life, we will all have a multitude of friendships.

Eros is the love most portrayed in movies, T.V. shows, and social media. Eros is all about romantic and sexual desires. A type of love we all desire to have and maintain with our significant others.

Agape is the love that seems hard to embrace fully. Learning to love all unconditionally has been a journey for me. It was a struggle to learn to love those who did me wrong or looked down on me because of who I was (and am) as a person. In my eyes, agape has been the hardest of the four loves.

So, I ask you this - can one love others genuinely, honestly, or sincerely when they don't genuinely love themselves?

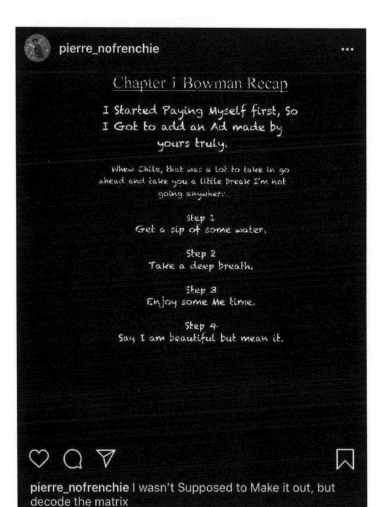

pierre_nofrenchie   •••

Chapter 1 Bowman Recap

I Started Paying Myself first, So
I Got to add an Ad made by
yours truly.

Whew Chile, that was a lot to take in go
ahead and take you a little break I'm not
going anywhere.

Step 1
Get a sip of some water.

Step 2
Take a deep breath.

Step 3
Enjoy some Me time.

Step 4
Say I am beautiful but mean it.

pierre_nofrenchie I wasn't Supposed to Make it out, but
decode the matrix

LOVE DESTROYS FEAR

I understand certain situations are out of our control but we must not let those types of events stunt our growth or the potential to become great. We must not "merely hope, for hope is like wishing upon a star (waiting for something to happen) but faith is the word we are looking for because we will muster up the strength to build our rocket ship (building a rocket ship is having the determination to work hard and not give up so that you can receive your blessings) to get to that shooting star.

Having the belief that our Love will conquer any obstacle that we are faced with will defeat the preconceived notion of fear. Yes, we may be hurting and dazed and confused but that pain shall pass. Going and growing through that pain can build something magnificent. It can create a more positive and fulfilling life for yourself after turning your negatives into positives. I may not be where I want to be in life but I'm working to achieve my dreams. I'm taking it a step at a time. With my newfound mindset I am living my life in my dream city, Miami, FL doing what I love, going to school and learning while spreading positivity.

Look at it like this… with the faith and courage to stay committed to Love, overcoming these obstacles will shape and mold you into someone who's able to share the pain. Sharing the pain allows you to help others escape the endless cycle of fear, which is us just spewing out our insecurities. These experiences will allow you to appreciate your Love for yourself and others because you now have the knowledge to not take things for granted and you don't want anyone to ever go through what you have gone through. And that's the beauty in the madness.

My past hardships, demons, traumas, and breakups have forced me to not only love myself unconditionally but to love others unconditionally. These experiences have allowed me to overcome my fears of self-hate and gave me the awe moment in life because Love has given me a purpose in life. That awe moment was when I realized I needed to not focus my time and energy on experiences out of my control. That I must try my hardest to stay positive and lead with a loving heart no matter how hard things got. Love has shown me that I don't need to fear death. We are all ticking time bombs, and I am not afraid of dying anymore. Death motivates me because I don't have much time on this earth. So, with all my heart, I will cherish every moment that passes me by. With the short amount of time I do have, I will use my Love to uplift a generation and inspire them to do remarkable things and live happier lives. I will use my Love to create the family I always wanted, and I look forward to that day when I will have a beautiful wife and kids. But until that happens, I will continue to build and perfect my rocket ship because my time is coming soon, and I must be ready when that opportunity presents itself. I urge you to use every moment to help build yourself up, so you too, can become the ultimate lover.

<u>LOVE IS DIVINE</u>

All it takes is effort to reaching divine love.
IM GOING TO BE POSITIVE FOR ONE SECOND
HOW ABOUT FOR ONE MINUTE
SHOOT IMMA TRY ONE HOUR
WAIT HOW ABOUT ONE DAY
WOW, I'M AT A WEEK
LET'S MAKE THIS TWO WEEKS
YOOO IT'S ALREADY A MONTH
DAMN LOOK AT THAT IT'S BEEN A YEAR
I'M LIKING THIS; IMMA DO THIS FOR LIFE
EFFORT IS ALL I ASK
IT'S NOT LIKE IM TRYING TO GET YOU TO ROB
A BANK WITH ME

DON'T THANK ME, THANK GOD,
AND SPREAD THE LOVE

Learning to Become Great

Martin Luther King Jr. planted the seed of bravery in me at an early age and now, fifteen years later, it is my turn to continue this tradition. I have faith that my book, through my past experiences, will inspire people to live braver lives. I hereby forthwith take a stand that my future actions will be a testament to this tradition.

VULNERABILITY

MANY SEE VULNERABILITY AS WEAKNESS;
I SEE IT AS YOUR GREATEST ALLY.

My first taste of vulnerability (I didn't even know what vulnerability meant at the time) happened in my English class in my junior year. To me, being vulnerable is being open and not afraid of what the outcome may be when sharing your love to others and realizing being transparent can help. It was the first week of school, and my family and I were still grieving the death of my grandfather. Our first assignment was to talk about an influential figure in our life. I immediately wrote about my granny because throughout the whole process of losing the love of her life, she remained faithful and committed to the Lord. She still managed to love everyone and smile. I was enamored by her resiliency. Not only did I have to write about her strength but I had to present the paper in class. I couldn't finish presenting it; I broke down. The eruption of tears came after stuttering over some words. I cried so much that my professor started crying, and to be frank, my paper wasn't all that good grammatically. I was not too fond of grammar and struggled in English. I knew in my heart that my essay wasn't "A" material but that's what I got. I even overheard a girl say: "He only got an A because he cried!"

(HATER!).

Learning to Become Great

God and the Universe decided to test me again, it was another moment in life I will never forget. That time I understood the word and the power it possessed. God tests us so we can share our TESTimony. I was with a group of people talking about the negative connotation of sex, on the first day when we had an opportunity to introduce ourselves. I shared my molestation with them that night. Initially I was afraid to speak my truth but I followed my instincts. I had made the commitment to let go of my dark truth. It was time for me to let my story be heard. Three days later when it was time for us to reflect on our weekend, three people spoke up about their own traumas.

Hearing me share my story gave them the power to speak up and overcome their pain and fears. I felt so much joy that I broke out crying. God was showing me the BEAUTY IN THE MADNESS. I was able to help, not knowing my choice would impact someone's life.

We are a very superficial society and we often fail to realize we have more things in common than not. We must make a conscious effort to help uplift each other. No one should believe that they must hold onto their pain because it's only their pain.

I once thought holding pain in was the right way to deal with it but I realized it wasn't right for my health. One day I decided that I would stop running from my demons and I sought help. Yes, I've been to therapy but only because I learned to become vulnerable, and my mentor told me I should seek treatment. Honestly, that has been one of the most phenomenal choices in my life, and I haven't looked back. I also don't let my past demons control me or use them as an excuse for not being the best self I can be. We can't control what happens outside of us, but we can control our emotional state and how we react. Let's set aside our differences and stand together to help uplift each other.

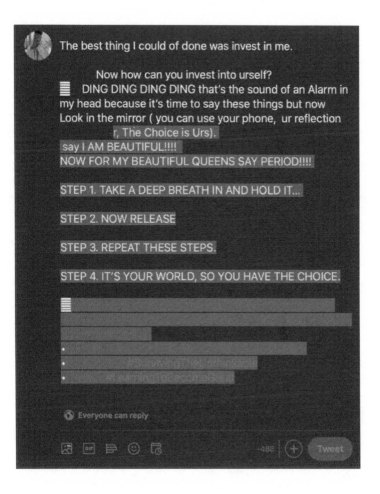

The best thing I could of done was invest in me.

Now how can you invest into urself?
DING DING DING DING that's the sound of an Alarm in my head because it's time to say these things but now Look in the mirror (you can use your phone, ur reflection r, The Choice is Urs).
say I AM BEAUTIFUL!!!!
NOW FOR MY BEAUTIFUL QUEENS SAY PERIOD!!!!

STEP 1. TAKE A DEEP BREATH IN AND HOLD IT...

STEP 2. NOW RELEASE

STEP 3. REPEAT THESE STEPS.

STEP 4. IT'S YOUR WORLD, SO YOU HAVE THE CHOICE.

Everyone can reply

There are 24 hours in a day and,
you taught me how to use
the most of my time Long Live
Kobe "Bean" Bryant!

R.I.P.

Payton Chester, Sarah Chester,
Alyssa Altobelli, Keri Altobelli,
John Altobelli, Christina Mauser,
& Ara Zobayan

Hey Big Head

I am a firm believer that we are given many talents in life but we must not take them for granted. Talent can only take us so far; without hard work, our abilities are limited.

During my freshman year in high school, I didn't make the fall football team, which angered me. When spring ball came around, I had a point to prove. By then we had a new head coach and atmosphere. My opportunity to prove myself was against Ryan Lankford, the greatest athlete (in my opinion), to go to our school. He was playing receiver and I was playing corner, we were in cover three (which means if you were to break the football into thirds, 1/3 of the field was my responsibility). I played off coverage (about five yards in front of the receiver). Honestly, I didn't know who Ryan was as a player before that moment. After being cut in the fall, I didn't go to any of the games.

Ryan ended up running a Go route. A go route is where you run straight, then try to outrun the corner. I immediately turned and burned, running as fast as possible. Ryan wasn't slowing down. Since nobody knew who I was as a football player, the quarterback and Ryan saw me as bait, so they targeted me.

We were running stride for stride when I noticed the ball was in the air. What they didn't know was I could jump higher than most. I ended up out jumping Ryan and intercepted the ball doing a 180 in the air as I was landing. To me, it was just another play, but as soon as I got to the sideline everyone was like," Yo, do you know who that was you just guarded." I shrugged, and they continued, "that's Ryan Lankford; he's a D1 player."

From that moment, I had the attention of the coaching staff. Later during spring try-outs, the junior varsity coaches asked: "Hey Freshman, why didn't you try out in the fall?" I was like, "Sir, I did try-out. You cut me." All they could say was: "My bad." The rest was history. My JV coaches gave me the nickname Baby Deion (what's crazy is he's my favorite NFL player of all time). I was able to show everyone that I was good at football. Coach Willie Offord, the head coach, was one of the first to notice my potential. It was one particular moment where he warned the upperclassmen, that even though I was undersized, I had talent.

My sophomore year came, and I started the season on JV but once the season finished, I was moved up to varsity. Before that happened, Coach O called me to his office. I had never been so nervous and intimidated in my life. My love for football was immense and I was about to find out if I was going to play varsity. I entered the room, and there were two coaches in the room but I was mainly focused on Coach O. Let me paint a picture of Coach O for you; he was around six foot one and had as much muscle as actor Terry Crews. This man had bigger calf muscles than my head. What scrawny kid wouldn't be intimidated? I walked in the room, and he laughed. It wasn't a regular laugh, it was an evil laugh (muahaha).

"Bowen what makes you think you should be on Varsity."

Me being super nervous I was like, "Ummm … Ummm. Because I am good."

He started to laugh even more and said: "Sophomore, I'm just busting your balls."

I had a moment of relief and was proud about what I just accomplished, not only did I make varsity I was able to follow my idol's (Deion Sanders) footsteps; I was given number two. It's a big deal to wear a single-digit number in high school, let alone wear it as an underclassman. I ended up finishing the season on a strong note.

Things got interesting my junior year; Coach O ended up stepping down and Coach Lundy who was the offensive coordinator took over, he too saw the raw talent I had. I was one of the most athletic kids on the field. He came up to me after one summer practice and told me his plans for me. He believed I had the talent to be better than Ryan Lankford and I felt so honored to be mentioned in the same sentence as him. Coach Lundy wanted me to play receiver, corner, punt return, kick return, gunner, and kick-off. My job was to be on the field at all times. He wanted me to step up and become a leader. I was a junior and it was time for me to continue to do what my Big Bro Ryan did before he left for the University of Illinois.

I failed miserably, and it wasn't for the lack of talent. It was because I got the Big Head. I stopped working hard because I thought I made it. And you couldn't tell me anything. I was the new man on the block and I had everyone in my corner. My name ended up becoming Marcus, "Look MA No Hands" Bowen. I had lost all the confidence in my ability to play the game I loved. I was able to get out of the doghouse but it wasn't the same. I didn't have that fire anymore. I was tainted. I went from having everything to losing everything because I didn't know how to stay at the top.

I ended up graduating high school and joining the military. While in the military, I gained a new hobby and that was basketball. Playing basketball on my base team while stationed at Cannon Air Force Base showed me how not to let my gifts go to waste. I didn't grow up playing basketball as a serious sport. I never worked on the art of the sport. It wasn't until my mentor, Ryan McGovern urged me to try out for the team. The base team would travel around to play other military teams. Ryan saw my athleticism and heart. But, as a basketball player, I was trash can. I didn't know how to shoot, dribble, and was uncoordinated. It was very humbling. I wasn't naturally gifted at it, and that brought something out of me that football didn't. Basketball brought out this alter ego; this new Marcus wasn't afraid of anyone. This Marcus didn't take no shit. This Marcus was uber aggressive and willing to do anything to win. I would purposefully get under people's skin.

But the best thing I got out of basketball was the brotherhood. Being the youngest and least talented on the team, I was like a baby shark thrown into a bigger ecosystem with even bigger sharks. Either I whine or I grow up and fight for what's mine, because truthfully, I don't like being trashcan at something. I worked my butt off and spent countless hours working on my craft, and whenever I had a question, I would ask one of my brothers.

I worked so hard that the best player on the team would often train me (Coach Mo, Ryan Lankford, Terrence Jackson, Ray King, Jamar Graham, Luis Ortiz). I was so dedicated to basketball that by year three, I became a captain, and it wasn't because of newly found talent. It was because of my work ethic and the heart and desire to get better. Looking back at the whole experience, I am incredibly grateful that my football career ended prematurely. And I'm incredibly blessed that I had the opportunity to play basketball.

One day it clicked as I was reflecting on my life. By year four, I started getting better at basketball, and many were surprised. I asked myself: "what if I put that same energy into a craft I was talented in?" I had put so much work into basketball, and the results were satisfying. I started implementing that mentality in everything I did in life, and I haven't looked back.

When you get that ounce of success, it's not the moment to relax and say, "Oh, I made it." That's a sign that you must work even harder to maintain your new success, and you must work even harder than that to achieve new heights of success.

Failing my teammates as a leader showed me that a true leader leads by example, and by working hard consistently no matter the situation. Talent only takes you so far and skill is useless if you don't back it with hard work. If you aren't giving everything you do in life your best, you will come up short every time. Don't be mad if your crops don't show because you failed to water them. Getting the big head will be your ultimate demise.

DRUGS

THERE ARE DRUGS WE ARE TAKING THAT WE DON'T EVEN REALIZE WE ARE CONSUMING.

Complaining and being cynical are Drugs. We all know someone who loves complaining or being negative no matter what. Have you ever considered that that person is that way because they are addicted to complaining and being negative? It's a different type of high but it's still a good high for them. They keep coming back for more and more, not even realizing they are stuck in this endless cycle of negativity. Their drug of choice is complaining or negativity. I was once stuck in that cycle, and it took a toll on my body.

Negativity and complaining drains your energy, and when I was in that cycle, no matter how much sleep I got, I was always tired and continuously had migraines. And when you are addicted to something, you fail to realize the root cause and tend to blame others and things outside of you. It all comes back to self. Until you take ownership or change your perspective, you will continue on a destructive path; allowing negativity to weaken your immune system, drain your body and cause unwarranted stress. We must not focus on the band-aid but focus on the wound.

My wound was being molested by my best friend, and everything else was a by-product (the band-aid). My form of negativity was to run far away from the primary source of my problems. It was like murdering someone and thinking I wouldn't get caught eventually. It was believing that ultimately, the problem would go away, and I could live the fairy tale ending but boy I was wrong. Every time something terrible happened, I solely focused on the situation (the band-aid) when I should have focused on why and how things transpired.

One particular area pops up in my head. I am advocating Vulnerability so here we go. And honestly, what I'm about to tell you is funny, so get ready to laugh at my pain. Every relationship I had with a woman started the same. If I liked a girl, whether it be physically, emotionally, spiritually, or intellectually, my phallus would be on ten on sight. In my head, I would be like, "Oh yeah, she about to get that work."

Yes, I was living in a state of ignorance. But, hey, life is about realizing what you were doing is ignorant and making a conscious effort to fix things. When things would escalate, and it was time for me to have intercourse (back when I had an immature mindset). I had become the "Boy with the Disappearing Phallus." EMBARRASSING and humbling at the same time.

Learning to Become Great

I had suppressed my traumatic experience believing that it would go away if I simply forget about it, the molestation. But, that didn't work. Instead, I thought I was cursed. It's like when an alcoholic gets treatment for alcohol abuse. It isn't the alcohol that's the problem, that's the band-aid. The real problem is the demon you are trying to escape by consuming that drink. I would be doing the same thing, but, for me, it was Mr. Squiggles (my phallus).

I eventually realized my disappearing phallus troubles started going away as I confronted my demons; and whooping their ass Naruto (anime character) style. I told my demons they couldn't live in my crib rent-free anymore. They had to get out.

Now I can honestly look back and laugh at the situation. Free at last! Free at last!

Create Post ×

CHAPTER 5

o   Ahahah I thought I finished my book, but I was blessed with this Idea

    Go Check MY TWEET THAT I POSTED ON 08/16/2020

•   https://twitter.com/bowman002/status/1294899975340675074?s=21

•   NOW LOOK AT THE TIME I POSTED IT ON EASTERN TIME THOUGH

o   CRAZY HUH GOOGLE THAT TIME

o   U SEE WHAT I DID?

o   PRAISE SWEET BABY JESUS

o   DEEP BREATHS U THOUGHT I FORGOT

STEP 1. TAKE A DEEP BREATH IN AND HOLD IT...
STEP 2. NOW RELEASE
STEP 3. REPEAT THESE STEPS.
STEP 4. IT'S YOUR WORLD SO YOU HAVE THE CHOICE.

    Take a 10 minute break
•   TAG ME ON IG & Twitter @ Pierre_NoFrenchie
•   With the #SurvivingTheUnthinkable
    And #LearningToBecomeGreat
    AND LET ME KNOW WHAT YOU LIKE BEST.

TWITTER.COM

Pierre_NoFrenchie on Twitter

"I WANT THE WORLD TO KNOW I LOVE GOD. NO MATTER WHAT HAPPENS IN LIFE I WANNA LET U KNOW YOU CAN OVERCOME UR...

Create Room   Photo/Video

NOT ALL DRUGS ARE BAD!

By the grace of GOD, I finally came to the realization that I was causing all this hurt upon myself. I was addicted to negativity, which was taking a toll on my body. So, I started taking a drug called positivity, and I can tell you my life took a complete one-eighty kickflip. The more I started taking this drug; the more I was able to love myself and the more energy my body had. This drug was also causing my headaches to go away.

I never had so much power in my life. That's when I was awakened to the truth that when I was addicted to negativity, my body was sending me signals (alarms) that I wasn't living the right way. I was like a depleted battery, a broken-down car, which was still trying to perform life tasks at an elevated level. And I'm here to tell you living in that state is very detrimental. I put it like this, if you were to go two months without feeding your pet fish; that fish would most likely die. Now, imagine not feeding that negativity for TWO MONTHS. I bet you that negativity will start to die off.

But it's easier said than done because your body has become addicted to the negativity and you will have moments where you relapse. You're going to want to revert to your old ways because it's comfortable. But we are resilient people, so, with faith and dedication, we can overcome and prosper.

I don't have the time nor the energy to complain or be negative because I know what toll it takes on my body. And you shouldn't devote any more time to negativity either. Use my past mistakes as learning tools, so you don't get addicted to negativity and complaining.

I was accepted into the "Cardiovascular Perfusion Program at Barry University." Changing my way of thinking was working and life was going great. I was getting the results I wanted. Then a pandemic! Due to COVID-19, my program was canceled. The only reason I moved to Miami was because of that program.

I was hurt initially because I had left the military and chased one of my many dreams. I thought becoming a perfusionist was a part of my destiny. A perfusionist is a technician who works on the heart and lung bypass machine that supplies the body with oxygen while the patient is in open heart surgery. But God was like, "Nah playboy, what I have for you is greater than what you want." What's crazy is not once did I complain about the program being canceled. My faith in God's plan is IMMENSE.

If I was still craving NEGATIVITY, I wouldn't have the motivation to tell you this story now; I would have made excuses and waited to write about my life. I grew up believing I was a terrible writer because I struggled with

English for most of my life but my professor, Mrs. Dominique Dieffenbach showed me that I have a voice and I am capable of writing. I just had to believe in myself and put forth the effort. SO, BE THE CHANGE NOW. By waiting you fall into the trap of getting some more of that fix of negativity. Time waits for no one.

We lash out Because of our demons, so we must realize that and put an end to the viscous cycle.

Dandelion

Pierre Bowen
Dominique Dieffenbach
ENC1101
23 Sept 2019

I want to start a movement to help subdue crime in the city that raised me. I want to be able to get kids off the streets and give them something no one can take from them, and that is knowledge. I would like to create a festival that will have music, food, vendors, and motivational speakers to drive home the point of nonviolence. I hope that I will be able to have a team to do this with me, for everyone brings something different to the table. Someone must step up and save these precious souls but I understand that this will not be an easy task. But through the grace of GOD, anything can be accomplished, showing them that one doesn't have to be famous to make a difference, to help build and create a better environment for our future generations. One day I will accomplish this; however, I would like this movement to be bigger than just Jacksonville. Always strive and prosper is the motto.

YOU CAN'T PUT UNLEADED GAS IN A FERRARI

Just like you have to put premium gas in a Ferrari, you should do things that help maintain and better your body. And sometimes we fall victim to becoming complacent. I also believe we fail to realize how amazing our bodies are. Once you know that, you too will want to treat your body as a Ferrari.

Once I started taking that drug called positivity, God, and the Universe started working in my favor, I would meet people and learn new things to help better my life. But you must be willing to learn and seek these opportunities with an open mind. Positive vibes only had become my way of life; and everything good that fell into place was just a by-product of my actions. Meditation was part of my fuel. When I initially tried meditating, I didn't have the right mindset. I would fall asleep. Food was also a byproduct of my new positive life. I had to choose something to eat that complimented the positivity I was taking in spiritually and mentally. I had to be open to giving up some foods and trying others even if I thought they were nasty - for example, coconut water. I was not too fond of the taste of it. With an open mind I grew to like the taste of coconut water. I decided to try these things without quitting. And I haven't looked back since. Each day I can honestly say I'm making progress on bettering myself.

I grew up hating vegetables and didn't eat much fruit. As my life turned for the better, I changed my perspective on fruits and vegetables and opened my mind. These foods tasted better once I changed my mindset. It's crazy how one slight change can have a domino effect. I now make a conscious effort to drink a homemade smoothie every day. I know deep down my body thanks me for it, and in return, my body will do its best to perform optimally.

Twenty years from now, I will honestly know if treating my body as a Ferrari has worked or not. For now, I can say my changes have worked. I'll repeat it, the key to all of this is; one must be open to trying new things and realize some of the old stuff isn't working. Why keep doing something if it hasn't garnered the results you wanted?

I've stumbled upon things that I thought I would never do as a kid growing up, things like meditation, yoga, and sound therapy. You must put premium gas in a Ferrari, and those things, in my opinion, are top-notch gas. Those things have changed my life tremendously because my problems like my headaches and my chronic fatigue slowly went away. I know for a fact that I have barely scratched the tip of the surface. Because of these practices, I'm able to live in a state of tranquility.

Learning to Become Great

We Are Kings & Queens

01001100
01101111
01110110
01100101
00100000

**WANNA KNOW WHAT THAT MEAN
CHECK MY IG POST ON FEBRUARY
23RD.**

INSTAGRAM IS PIERRE_NOFRENCHIE

Smoothies

Monday (yellow)
½ Cup Almond Milk
Greek Yogurt
Pineapple
Mango
Bananas

Tuesday (Orange)
½ cup Orange Juice
Greek Yogurt.
1 Orange
Peaches
Watermelon

Wednesday (PINK)
½ Cup Almond Milk
Greek yogurt
Watermelon
Strawberries
Raspberries

Thursday (Purple)
½ Cup Cranberry juice
Greek Yogurt
Blue Berries
Cherries

Friday (Green)
½ Cup Orange Juice
Greek Yogurt
Avocado
Kale
Kiwi
Apple

I am, and I will be wealthy in
spirit, soul, mind, body,
and pockets!

I am, and I will be wealthy in
spirit, soul, mind, body,
and pockets!

I am, and I will be wealthy in
spirit, soul, mind, body,
and pockets!

I am, and I will be wealthy in
spirit, soul, mind, body,
and pockets!

I am, and I will be wealthy in
spirit, soul, mind, body,
and pockets!

Smile, you are alive!
Smile, you are alive!
Smile, you are alive!

BLUETOOTH

WE HAVE BEEN CONDITIONED TO BELIEVE THAT WE MUST SEE THINGS TO KNOW THEY ARE WORKING IN OUR FAVOR.

We don't necessarily see Bluetooth technology working but we know it works once we connect our phone to our headphones. We also can't see the air we breathe but we know it works because we are alive. What I am trying to say is we must not lose confidence, instead we must maintain faith because we don't need to see things to know that GOD and the UNIVERSE are working in our favor.

Things will forever work in our favor if we are persistent, confident, dedicated, positive, prepared, and willing to work hard. Even when things seem like they aren't working in our favor, just know they are. Rejection is Divine redirection. We must be open and willing to be redirected for our betterment. The moment we give up is the moment we could have had a breakthrough. Always stay prepared because our time will come, and when it does, we must be ready to capitalize on it. Think about what you want to do in life and try your best - no matter how bad things may get - remember equanimity.

Learning to Become Great

When I first took anatomy and physiology, I was overwhelmed and ready to quit because it was new and foreign to me. I doubted myself and didn't think I could pass the class but I remembered nothing in life comes easy. So, I changed my mindset and continued to work hard to get an understanding of my classes. By forcing myself to get comfortable with being uncomfortable, I was able to get an A on every test I took. If I had listened to my initial thoughts; I would have dropped out of class like the guy who sat next to me and so many more that came before him. The moral of the story is; never give up just because something challenges you or makes you uncomfortable. If you do you would be blocking your unseen blessings.

Your defining moments in life are the moments you choose to fight for, instead of giving up when times get rough. I believe in you. But that statement holds no weight if you don't believe in yourself.

Make Today Great!
Make Today Great!
MAKE TODAY GREAT!
I am intelligent!
I am intelligent!
I AM INTELLIGENT!

HERE'S A LIL BOWMAN FACT
GIT IS THE PHOTOGRAPHER WHO'S RESPONSIBLE FOR MY BOOK COVER.
ON THE DAY I SCHEDULED MY PHOTO SHOOT,
I WAS AN HOUR LATE BECAUSE I LOCKED
MYSELF OUT OF MY CAR.
SO I RAN TO THE CVS OFF BLANDING AND COLLINS.
I USED THE CVS PHONE TO CALL MY MOM,
AND TOLD HER TO DM GIT.
BUT IG IS SETUP TO WHERE IF YOU DON'T FOLLOW THAT PERSON YOU ARE NOT GOING TO GET A NOTIFICATION, BUT GIT SO HAPPENED TO BE IN HIS DM'S
30 MINUTES LATER MY SUV FINALLY GOT UNLOCKED, AND I CALLED @IGIT SAYING," BRO IM SORRY... I KNOW YOU ARE A BUSY PERSON BUT LET'S CANCEL IM STILL GOING TO PAY YOU. SORRY FOR WASTING YOUR TIME".
GIT SHOWED NOTHING BUT LOVE AND LOOK WHAT WE CREATED WORKING WITH EACH OTHER

SEE FOR YOUR SELF.

**OUR PODCAST IS COMING SOON
AND CAN I PLEASE HEAR YOUR SIDE OF THE
STORY IM TRYING TO SEE SOMETHING.**

Breadcrumbs

Everything must start from within, and you must be brutally honest with yourself, because everything comes back to self. Once I started looking at life from that perspective, breadcrumbs (breadcrumbs are the little clues I used to help me figure out what my purpose in life was) began popping up everywhere. It was up to me to reflect on my life and piece things together. One of the first crumbs was when I was nine years old and in second grade for the second time (almost a year after I was a molested). A teacher who never taught me came up to me and asked: "Why are you always smiling?" I told her I didn't know. And I didn't know then but now I understand it was because no matter how hard life gets, I must continue to shine my light and stay faithful to God. Since that moment, I was able to realize the power of a smile and that you don't know who you are influencing in life (someone is always watching). We must stay open and realize that kids and people younger than us can teach us valuable lessons in life.

Another critical point in my life was when my Grandfather was on his death bed. I was 17 and still lost in the world, but it was one moment in life that I would never forget. My Grandfather had transitioned to hospice (in his own home), and the whole family was there. We all were in the front room and my grandmother told me: "Your grandfather wants to speak to you." I was baffled, and, in my mind, I started questioning why me?

He grabbed my hand and said: "Jr let's escape, you and I. Let's get out of here and travel the world. Son, please help me get rid of this pain so we can get out of here." Years later I'm still trying to decipher that moment. What I did get from that is he saw something special in me, something I didn't see in myself until I learned to defeat my demons. He died a week after that moment.

Then random but not-so-random moments started popping up in my life after my Grandfather's death. I say not-so-random because I don't believe in coincidences anymore. Everything serves a purpose in life. My next you-are-a-special-kid occurrence happened in the spring of 2011. It was my first week on the job as a cashier at McDonald's. An older, frail, white man with gray hair, wearing a dirty white t-shirt and carrying a plastic bag came in. I perceived him to be homeless and crazy. He stood in the middle of the lobby, looked me directly in my eyes, pointed at me and said: "You are special." I felt exactly how I felt when I was with my Grandfather. Again, I was in a state of why and how. That was the last and only time I saw that homeless man.

Seven years later, I was 24 and in the military. I would have meaningful talks with one of my co-workers who held a higher rank than I. He was the next person to say there was something special about me and he was the first person I told about the breadcrumb analogy. Our first encounter was a tone-setter. He walked up and said: "Bowen, I heard through the grapevine you are a slacker." I proceeded to say: "I don't care what people think of me." I briefly paused. You could see the disappointment on his face but after my brief pause, I said: "I don't care because at the end of the day, I still have to show up and work to the best of my ability." His disappointment turned into astonishment. That brief dialogue allowed us to have countless number of conversations.

Two of my neighbors; Sugarmeat and McLovin, who were more like extended family had always seen something in me as well. They introduced me to an entrepreneur who could help point me in the right direction with one of my ideas. The two of us ended up scheduling a business meeting at Starbucks. I thought it would only last thirty minutes but it lasted around two hours. It's funny how life works sometimes. We weren't just talking about my future business ideas. He told me how to improve myself. An hour into the meeting before I even told him about my ultimate goal of starting a non-profit and giving back to the community, he said:" You probably heard this before but I'm not sure."

My mind jumped to those moments with my Grandfather and the homeless man. He looked at me and continued, "Marcus, there's something about your aura/spirit, I can't quite put my finger on it, but you are unique." By then, I was foaming at the mouth, ready to tell him that I had heard that before multiple times. This time was different because I believed that I was exceptional, and the meeting was positive reinforcement that I was on the right track, and I was serving my purpose in life.

After finding my purpose in life, which is to give back to my community and help uplift a generation to make better decisions in life. I started to meet beautiful people who taught me so much about life in such a short amount of time. It was like God was putting angels in my path to teach me and remind me that I am on the right track and to keep fighting for what was right. And Over a span of a year, I had multiple occurrences with strangers who I felt like I have known my whole life. It always seemed like they would appear at the perfect time too.

For instance, I had this concept I had been designing for over three years, so I decided to take an art class. I didn't know any of the professors, so I randomly picked a class. I ended up choosing a 2D design course with Professor Dustin Harewood. From the moment, Professor Harewood stepped in the class with his pinecone and spoke about the importance of such an overlooked plant (pinecones protect and store pine tree seeds); I knew he would help take my design to the next level. He did just that and more by getting me to make slight tweaks to my design. And in my eyes, he's a true living legend because his lessons were more significant than just art. He taught me how to value myself on a deeper level and not to overlook the things that society may deem unworthy. His perspective caused me to view life in a completely new way. I don't take nature and colors for granted; instead, I enjoy their beauty.

He helped me reach a new level of creativity. His teachings showed me how to let my creativity flow and not to think too much, and that all I needed to do was follow my heart. I started to realize GOD was putting me in these situation-ships to train and ultimately "mold me into the man He wanted me to be. So, I urge you to reflect on life so you too, can start picking up those breadcrumbs to figure out what it is that God has instore for you. Once you do, teachers, in many forms, will begin to appear to help guide you in the right direction. Remember, the learning process will never end. Stay thirsty my friends!

WELL GOD AND THE UNIVERSE HAVE BEEN GIVING YOU ANSWERS ALL ALONG IN THE FORM OF LITTLE BREADCRUMBS BUT IT'S UP TO YOU TO PICK UP THESE BREADCRUMBS AND PIECE THINGS TOGETHER

We Are ON An ULTRALIGHT BEAM.

HOW ARE YOU FEELING MY BEAUTIFUL SOULS?

DO ME A FAVOR TAKE ANOTHER BREAK
YOU DESERVE IT
WHILE ON THAT BREAK DRINK SOME WATER
AND TAKE THOSE DEEP BREATHS

I HAVE ANOTHER EASTER EGG YOU READY

CHECK MY IG POST TIME STAMP
AUG 10,2013
PIERRE_NOFRENCHIE

INVESTING

THE BEST INVESTMENT IN LIFE IS INVESTING INTO THYSELF.

When you bet on yourself, you win every time if you put in the work. Don't expect to win if you didn't prepare yourself or set yourself up to win. Also, don't be afraid to get what's rightfully yours. I always like to say: "If one isn't living life on the edge, is he or she truly living a joyous life?" You can have whatever you desire in this life but that usually doesn't happen because we allow our doubt or others' doubt to deter us from getting ours. Or we tend to play it safe. It isn't a risk unless you don't put forth the determination and effort behind the pursuit of whatever your heart desires. Look at it like this when you do fail (and you will), don't look at it as a failure. What I mean is, it's GOD and the UNIVERSE showing you the weakness in your investment. Accept the defeat as a lesson, strengthen that weakness, and use your persistence.

Once again, you may be wondering how to get these answers, so you can start to invest in yourself. The more you invest in yourself, the more ideas you will get, and these ideas will help you create beautiful things. Take that leap of faith. I'll be by your side, cheering for you.

I WAS THE KID WHO TOUCHED A CACTUS, I WAS THE KID WHO SET THE TRASHCAN ON FIRE, I WAS THE KID WHO RODE A BIKE DOWN THE STAIRS, I WAS THE KID WHO TOUCHED A HOT IRON. I WAS ALSO THE KID WHO LEARNED FROM THOSE MISTAKES AND PROSPERED.

I failed second grade but I didn't let that stop me. Looking back on life, I often invested in things that weren't for my benefit. Materialistic items that didn't give me an "ROI" (return on investment). Shoes were one of my "Liabilities." Is looking fly an ROI? I'm not knocking shoes but building generational wealth is more important. I was making other people wealthy and chasing their dreams while forgetting about myself and my ambitions. There comes a time where you ask yourself: Am I investing in the right things? There's a term we must learn to practice - Delayed Gratification. Waiting and holding off on desires until generational wealth is established. Why buy a pair of shoes now when you can buy the store later? Invest into thyself - start a business based on your talents.

I did whatever it took to invest in self. And whenever I second-guessed myself, I reminded me that I never second-guessed buying shoes. I've spent over 10-thousand dollars on tennis shoes. And yes, I understand you can flip shoes but that's not the point I'm trying to teach. For me it's shoes; for you it could be alcohol. Spending on something with no return instead of saving and investing is the point you need to consider.

The more you invest in yourself, the more ideas you will get, and these ideas will help you create beautiful art (art to me is everything you do in life). Take that leap of faith. I'll be by your side, cheering for you.

I own a real pair of OFF WHITE 1s
But I got greedy and tried getting a 2nd pair
and they ended up being fake.
So I just turned them into an Art piece.

I will uplift a generation
to do better.
I will uplift a generation
to do better.
I will uplift a generation
to do better.
I am great!
I am great!
I AM GREAT!
I Love Myself, I love myself,
I LOVE MYSELF!
I Love Myself, I love myself,
I LOVE MYSELF!

I Love Myself, I love myself,
I LOVE MYSELF!
I am Beautiful, I am beautiful, I
AM BEAUTIFUL!
I am Beautiful, I am beautiful, I
AM BEAUTIFUL!
I am Beautiful, I am beautiful, I
AM BEAUTIFUL!

WEIRDO

DON'T BE AFRAID TO LIVE YOUR TRUTH BECAUSE YOU THINK YOU WON'T FIT IN.

I always wondered how I was deemed weird, or why did people think I was weird. I lived in that internal struggle for most of my life until I realized that being weird wasn't my enemy but being weird was one of my greatest strengths. I stopped viewing my weirdness as kryptonite and started seeing it as Mike's secret stuff. My weirdness is my superpower. It's what makes me unique and special.

WE ARE ALL WINNERS JUST REMEMBER WE BEAT OUT MILLIONS OF SPERM CELLS!

There comes a time when you realize you must stop running away from yourself to live a life of true happiness. You are special and unique too. GOD and the UNIVERSE has gifted you with special powers only for you, so I advise you to embrace them and learn to become more vulnerable to live a life of unconditional Love. Learning to embrace my true self has opened doors I didn't even imagine seeing growing up. I have met so many beautiful people, and I will continue to meet fascinating people. Remember, you are perfect the way you are, and don't let society discourage you from living your authentic life.

I would get picked on because I was a virgin. I didn't lose my virginity until I was 22. People used to think I was gay. Honestly, I was afraid to love because of what had transpired when I was eight years old. I never understood why I was called weird because I was just me. Was it because I wasn't afraid to talk about random things? Was it because I had a different thought process? Was it because I wasn't scared to speak my truth? Or was it because I didn't fit the stereotypical black male they portray in the movies?

TEAM ABC STAND UP

I Love Myself, i love myself,
I LOVE MYSELF!

I Love Myself, i love myself,
I LOVE MYSELF!

I Love Myself, i love myself,
I LOVE MYSELF!

I am Beautiful, i am beautiful,
I AM BEAUTIFUL!

I am Beautiful, i am beautiful,
I AM BEAUTIFUL!

I am Beautiful, i am beautiful,
I AM BEAUTIFUL!

Free At last Free at Last

I's Tired MASTA

I'S TIRED OF JUST BEING

LOOKED AT AS A THUG

AS A DRUG DEALER

AS AN ATHLETE

AS AN OVERLY AGGRESSIVE MALE

AS A STATISTIC

AS A SEX TOY

AS A DUMMY

AS A DEMON

AS An ENTERTAINER

I'S SICK AN TIRED OF BEING LOOKED AT AS
LESS THAN HUMAN

THE REVOLUTION WILL START ON SOCIAL
MEDIA

I'S COMPASSIONATE

I AM INTELLIGENT

I AM GIFTED

I AM A HUMAN BEING JUST LIKE YOU

Hey Everybody

IT'S NOT ME THEY FEAR
IT'S MY SKIN THEY FEAR
CAN YOU HEAR ME
BUT THEY WANT ME TO HANG
FROM THE POPLAR TREE
LIKE A STRANGE FRUIT
BUT I GET ON A KNEE
AND PRAY TO THE LORD
TO SET ME FREE

HOW WAS THE JOURNEY?
CHECK OUT MY TWEET I HAVE MADE UP MYMIND
ON THE WHOLE JAY-Z OR MONEY DECISION.
BUT TO FIND OUT
GO CHECK OUT MY TWEET
LET ME MAKE IT EASYFOR YOU

Goals to A Healthy Lifestyle

It all started when I had a conversation with a couple of friends about my future goals. They explained the importance of writing things down and holding myself accountable to completing the things I had written. I decided to put my ideas in the form of a list. It housed ideas that I could possibly use to teach and help uplift youth. It is also what I practice to better myself and in return I can use my results to show how these things can be beneficial in life.

So, I come to you today because the time is now to make a change, and this is a start. Life is all about planting seeds, and I can't plant them all. I can't change the world alone, so join me in changing this world. We have unique abilities, and when we team up, we can do even greater things in this life for our future generations. We must create a safe and healthy world for our future generations. We need to protect the EARTH.

Life Skills
- How to Fix Cars?
    - Changing Flat Tires
    - Rotate Tires
    - Oil Change
- How to find a Job?
    - Research
    - Internships
    - Résumé
    - Employee Values

63

- How to Create a Business?
    - Real Estate
    - Stock Market
    - Your own Personal Business
- How to Improve Communication?
    - Build Confidence
    - Eye Contact
    - Be Precise
- How to cook?
    - Healthy recipes
    - Google
    - YouTube
    - Practice
- Manage Money
    - Financial Education
    - Debt/ Income Ratio
    - Investing
    - Retirement Funds
    - Taxes

What is Success?

- Make success Your Own
    - Invest in Yourself
    - Grind Hard
    - Take Your Time
    - Don't Get Discouraged
    - Don't Take Short Cuts
    - Give Back to Your Community
    - Then Give Back to the world
    - Learn from Others
    - God Blessed Talents

Learning to Become Great

Education
- Take it seriously
- Hidden Scholarships
  - Talk to guidance Counselors
- Take Advance College courses
- Importance of Education
  - Read books

Professionalism
- Dress for the business or job you want
- Mannerisms
- Confidence
- Positive Vibes
- Perception
- Posture
- Knowing what to say
- Knowing How to Carry Yourself

Feeding Your Love
- Meditation
- Thirst for knowledge
- Positivity
- Yoga
- Mantras
- Storge
- Philia
- Eros
- Agape
- Virtues

I also need your help making this list even better.

Email: yopierre@marcusbowen.net

IG: pierre_nofrenchie

Reach out to me so that we can create a Dialogue. I would love to hear what you thought about the book. I'm here with you. I'll be waiting.

Acknowledgements

My Love Letter to you

I'm on my J Cole sh#% , so here we go. A personal shout out to GOD. I couldn't do any of this and I mean none of this without you. You're funny as hell, GOD but you my Dawg. To my three Beautiful Magnolia Flowers, Granny INEZ, Granny Mary-Ann, and MOMMY - "Hurricane Sharon" (don't beat me for that nick name) but thank y'all for being strict and praying for me, LORD knows I needed it. I wanna thank my big ole beautiful family; your impact on my life have been immense and y'all better be reading this in my voice. To my friends - stay thirsty mi amigos! To all of you whom I haven't had the chance to personally meet, I am beyond honored that you took the time out of your day to read what I had to say. And fam, I know it may come as a shock to find out some of the things that transpired but through GOD which is LOVE, thank you for always being by my side. To everybody, I wish you nothing but blessings. This is only phase one. I have big plans to give back to our communities and I can't do it alone. I have faith that we will stand together and continue to make changes in this world. And this portion wasn't edited because at the end of the day I am flawed and honestly, I don't want to because I have the power through GOD not to and I'm just talking right now but anyway …

I LOVE YOU GUYS!!!

I need your input to make the next version of this book and my future books better.

Please leave me an honest review on Amazon letting me know what you thought of the book.

Say Their Name

THEY DIDN'T HAVE THE OPPORTUNITY TO SPEAK THEIR TRUTH'S, SO IT'S OUR JOB TO SPEAK OURS
THEY ARE THE MODERN-DAY EMMETT TILL.
SLEEP ON THAT

ERIC GARNER - JOHN CRAWFORD III - MICHAEL BROWN - EZELL FORD - DANTE PARKER - MICHELLE CUSSEAUX - LAQUAN MCDONALD - GEORGE MANN - TANISHA ANDERSON - AKAI GURLEY - TAMIR RICE - RUMAIN

BRISBON - JERAME REID -
MATTHEW AJIBADE - FRANK SMART
-NATASHA MCKENNA - TONY
ROBINSON - ANTHONY HILL - MYA
HALL - PHILLIP WHITE - ERIC
HARRIS - WALTER SCOTT -
WILLIAM CHAPMAN II - ALEXIA
CHRISTIAN - BRENDON GLENN -
VICTOR MANUEL LAROSA -
JONATHAN SANDERS - FREDDIE
BLUE - JOSEPH MANN - SALVADO
ELLSWOOD - SANDRA BLAND -
ALBERT JOSEPH DAVIS - DARRIUS
STEWART - BILLY RAY DAVIS -
SAMUEL DUBOSE - MICHAEL SABBIE
- BRIAN KEITH DAY - CHRISTIAN
TAYLOR - TROY ROBINSON -
ASSHAMS PHAROAH MANLEY - FELIX
KUMI- KEITH HARRISON MCLEOD -
JUNIOR PROSPER - LAMONTEZ
JONES - PATERSON BROWN -
DOMINIC HUTCHINSON - ANTHONY

ASHFORD – ALONZO SMITH –
TYREE CRAWFORD – INDIA KAGER
– LA'VANTE BIGGS – MICHAEL
LEE MARSHALL – JAMAR CLARK –
RICHARD PERKINS – NATHANIEL
HARRIS PICKETT – BENNI LEE
TIGNOR – MIGUEL ESPINAL –
MICHAEL NOEL – KEVIN MATTHEWS
– BETTIE JONES – QUINTONIO
LEGRIER – KEITH CHILDRESS JR –
JANET WILSON – RANDY NELSON –
ANTRONIE SCOTT – WENDELL
CELESTINE – DAVID JOSEPH –
CALIN ROQUEMORE – DYZHAWN
PERKINS – CHRISTOPHER DAVIS –
MARCO LOUD – PETER GAINES –
TORREY ROBINSON – DARIUS
ROBINSON – KEVIN HICKS – MARY
TRUXILLO – DEMARCUS SEMER –
WILLIE TILLMAN – TERRILL
THOMAS – SYLVILLE SMITH –
ALTON STERLING – PHILANDO
CASTILE – TERENCE CRUTCHER –

PAUL O'NEAL – ALTERIA WOODS –
JORDAN EDWARDS – AARON BAILEY
– RONELL FOSTER – STEPHON
CLARK – ANTWON ROSE II –
BOTHAM JEAN – PAMELA TURNER –
DOMINIQUE CLAYTON – ATATIANA
JEFFERSON CHRISTOPHER
WHITFIELD – CHRISTOPHER
MCCORVEY – ERIC REASON –
MICHAEL LORENZO DEAN –
BREONNA TAYLOR
GEORGE FLOYD

Shout Outs

I want to thank the following businesses for helping me in the process:-

- FIGHT FOR JESS PLEASE SUPPORT THE EVER-BEAUTIFUL JESSICA FLORENCE. STAY STRONG AND BEAUTIFUL LOVE. FOLLOW HER ON INSTAGRAM AT geneva_la_jade;

- For marketing inquiries hit up my brother, Git Du Tran. He's one of the most creative people I've worked with. E-mail: info@weekthink.com;

- If you are ever in the Mendenhall, MS area and need a haircut from one of the best in Mississippi hit up my cousin Timothy Willis at "Willis Barbershop";

  - 116 Victory Rd, Mendenhall, MS 39114

- Derrick Florence a.k.a. Moonmanflo will definitely hit you with some intricate bars. He's on all streaming platforms;

- If you are ever in Vancouver, WA area and need your hairline blessed by the best barber in the area hit my boy Gian Jay Harris "Generations Barbershop";

- If you are ever in Duval, Jacksonville, FL and need a barber DM award-winning @luke_nahshin on Instagram;

Learning to Become Great

- If you ever need quality custom made jewelry check out Aviant Jewelers at aviantjewelers.com;

- If you ever need film production or photography, contact my family George and Illy at Filmrat Production. Filmratproductions@gmail.com;

- Whenever you need to listen to some inspiring words; check out my brother's podcast The MindOfJones and BurgToTheBay;

- When you are comfortable and need help with confronting the mental health stigma and generational traumas Candace D. Thompson and her company Candidcultureco is the spot to go to. Check out her website www.candidculture.org;

- Whenever you need some new flava in your ear, check out my soul brotha who is a multitalented artist known as Eddy Braveaux. He's on all streaming platforms;

- When you decide to write your book, play, or film script and need a writing coach or development editor, check out E. Claudette Freeman and her Literary Services team at www.pecantreebooks.com;

- If you are ever in need of Media Kits, brochures, magazines, and catalogs get in contact with The Hartley Press Commercial Printer;

- If you live in the Jax area and need On-Demand Tech Services hit up Sparc+ on Instagram at sparcplus. Their number and website is (904) 501-506 and www.sparcplus.tech;

- Do you wanna lift your soul and get a great workout in? H it up my highly motivated brotha Jackson Le at www.ltsfitness.com;

- Need some mood changing and ear questioning music? check out Hip-Hop artist Zach Flowers. He's on all streaming platforms;

- Check out my homie Christopher Davis a.k.a. thelillakerboy and his podcast at immortalmamba.com;

- Avery Junius my high school look alike if you need a professional photographer his Instagram is1takeace. His podcast is dope too.

- If you are hungry and want to try the Illest Chef in Jax contact the homie Kalin Anderson aka Sir Chef Naps at Feedtheville on Instagram.

- If you are in the mood to Rage and get lit go listen to my lil brother Billy Winfield he is streaming on all platforms

- Whenever you're in the mood for some two stepping smooth singing Gents check out the Duo Cho53n 1. They are on all streaming platforms;

- Need a loving soul to help you with social media marketing hit up the beautiful Jasmin Lankford on Instagram at jasmin_justlisten;

Learning to Become Great

- If you are in Jacksonville and need a haircut, go to my mentor, LoToice Walton at Restored Crowns located at:

  - 1021 Oak St Suite 131 Jacksonville, FL 32204;

  - He's also a certified professional inspector at LoToice Walton Home Inspections;

- Check out my mentor, Mgm Mike Mike, he's a talented Artist/Songwriter and his beats be knocking. His music is out now on all streaming platforms. Instagram is mgm_mikemike;

- Looking for inspiration for a teen or young adult? Consider the book BASSketball Lessons written to student- athletes (or honestly anyone) by Brent Bass. Find it on Amazon or listen to his concise bi-weekly podcast on ITunes by the same name.

- Go check out the ever beautiful Ebonique Brooks podcast called theauntiehousepod, she's an old soul trapped in a Young body expressing her elegant thoughts about the world she's living in.

- If you want to hear about sports go check out my brother Kendall Showers podcast called Hang My Jersey, it's out on all platforms.

About the Author

Aim for The Stars

As a kid growing up, Marcus Bowen always wondered how the greats like Michael Jordan, Kobe Bryant, Muhammed Ali, Manny Pacquiao, Kevin Hart, Jay-Z, Tom Brady, Lebron James, Will Smith, Quincy Jones, Deion Sanders, Jerry Rice, Peyton Manning (and the list goes on) maintained success at such a high level for most of their career. And as he studied them, he realized that their work ethic was bar none. He also noticed that not only was their work ethic elite, they didn't allow their hardships to define them. They used their troubling times as fuel to become even greater. Marcus Bowen, an Air Force veteran, shares his story and how he developed his tools to strive for greatness while overcoming hardships. It is one of his dreams to share his story to help others get all the greatness life holds for them too.

Life throws lemons at us often without providing water and sugar to turn them into lemonade. Through trial and error, we realize that one of the greatest lessons in life is to look at each experience as an opportunity to learn, to grow and to walk out your purpose.

Yet, you have to choose. Will you walk out your life in negativity? Will you walk your journey holding hands with darkness? Will you ignore the signs that your life is about something bigger than you?

Marcus Bowen transparently walks us through his choices and shares some thoughts and insight that he challenges you to employ to learn to not become better but to become great.

Made in the USA
Columbia, SC
28 June 2021